Every part of you

## turns me on.

Hand over this note, and I'll kiss every inch of your body.

W0037658

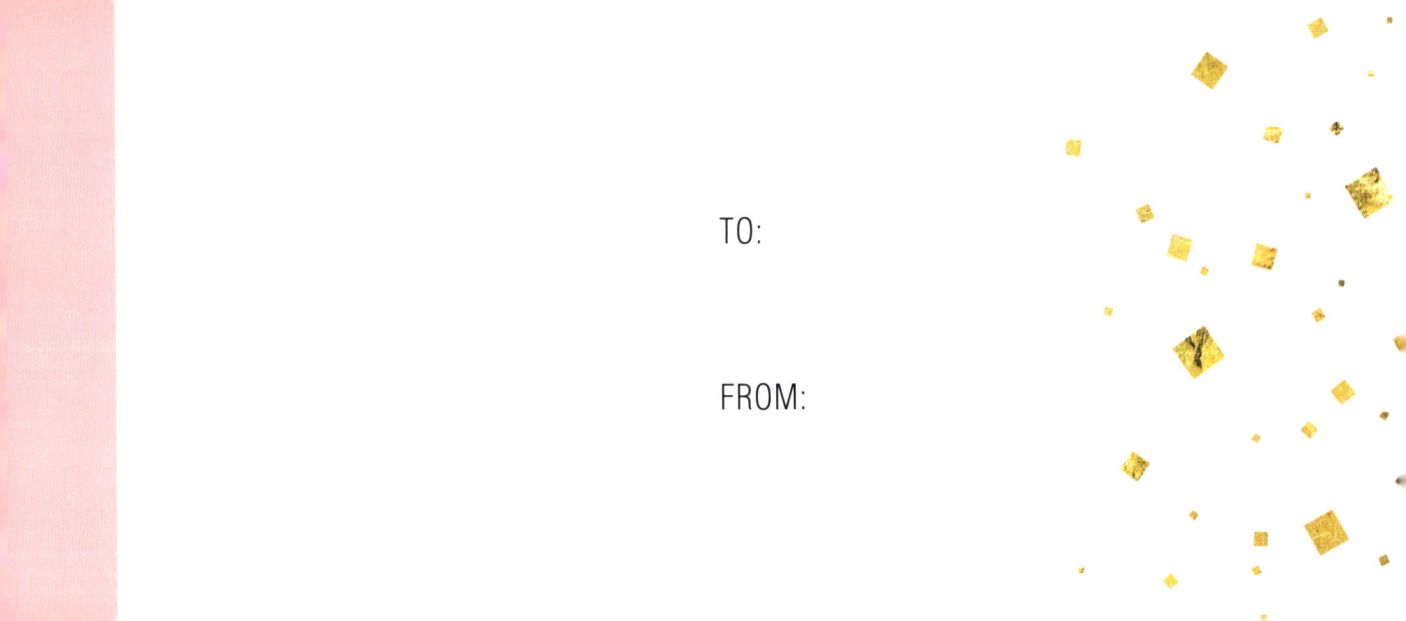

TO:

FROM:

You look

*unbelievably sexy*

anytime, anywhere, in anything.

TO:

FROM:

# redeem this note,

and I won't sway from that sweet spot until you beg me to.

TO:

FROM:

You are the absolute

*best kisser.*

Hand over this note to teach me a thing or two.

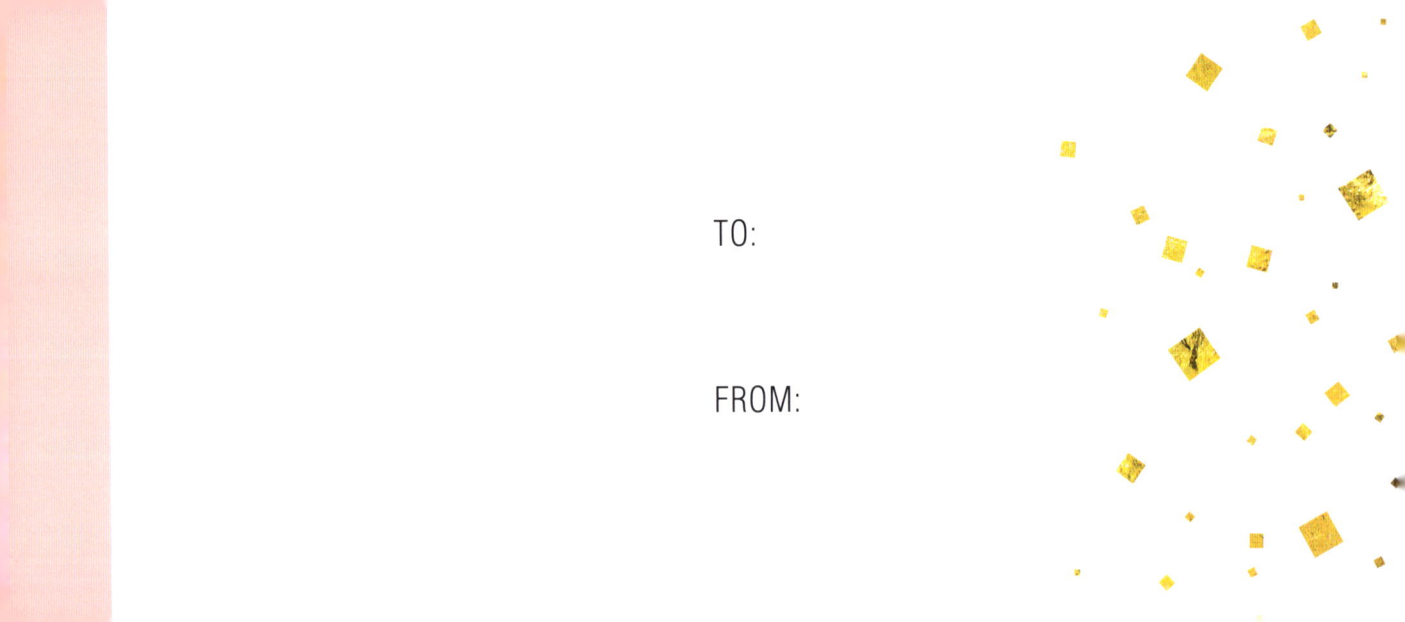

TO:

FROM:

Here's a little reminder that

*you're the sexiest*

person alive.

TO:

FROM:

## redeem this note

when you crave a foot massage—also good for other body parts.

TO:

FROM:

# Let's explore

that sexy imagination of yours.

Hand over this note to reenact your most private fantasy.

TO:

FROM:

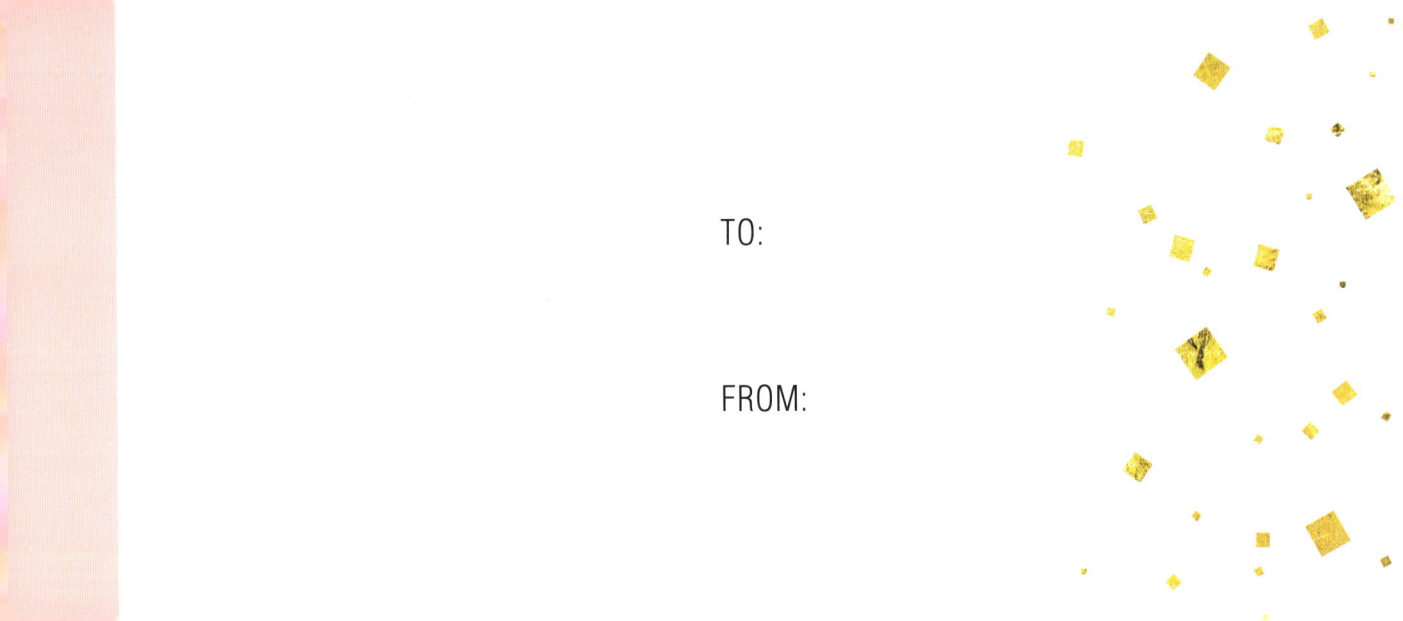

Just the

*thought of you*

turns me on.

TO:

FROM:

# redeem this note

for some hot and cold delights—think ice cubes and warm massage oil.

TO:

FROM:

You have the

*sexiest voice.*

Hand over this note and we'll read erotic poetry to each other over a bottle of wine.

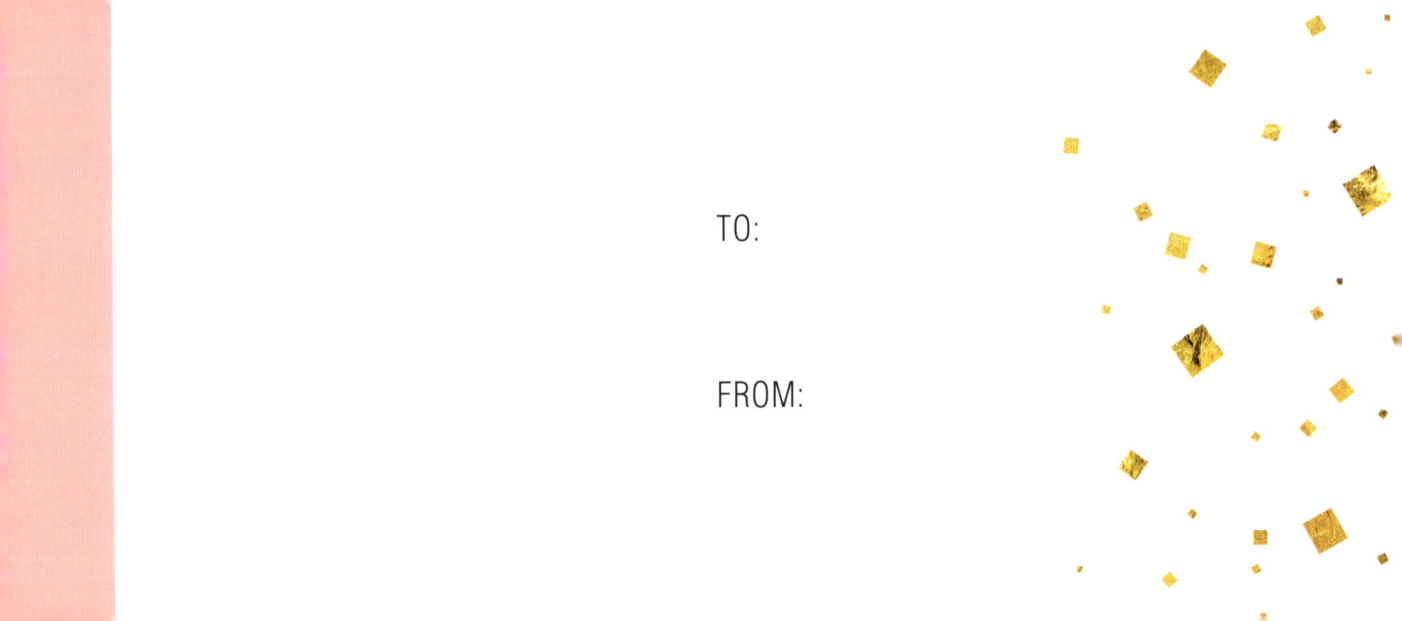

TO:

FROM:

Your eyes are

*the sexiest*

shade of _____ .

TO:

FROM:

# redeem this note

and we'll both drop what we're wearing, then and there.

TO:

FROM:

You've been

naughty.

Hand over this note and you'll get
some provocative punishment.

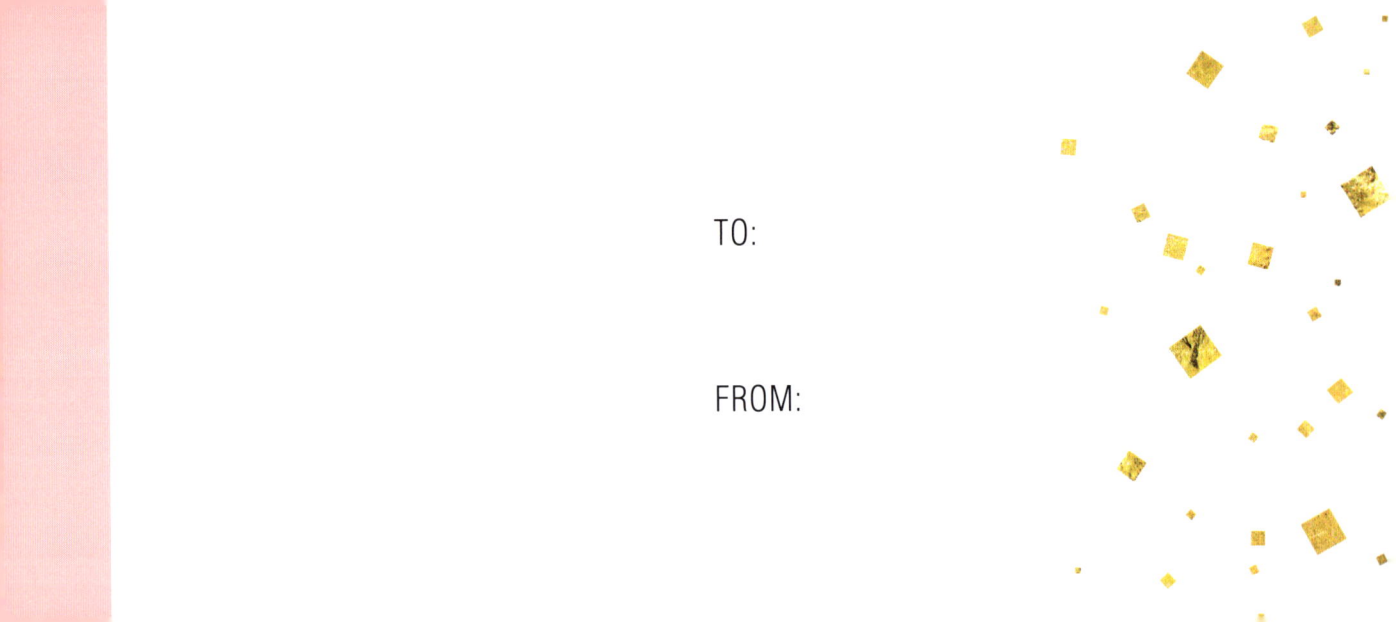

TO:

FROM:

You have the most

*kissable lips.*

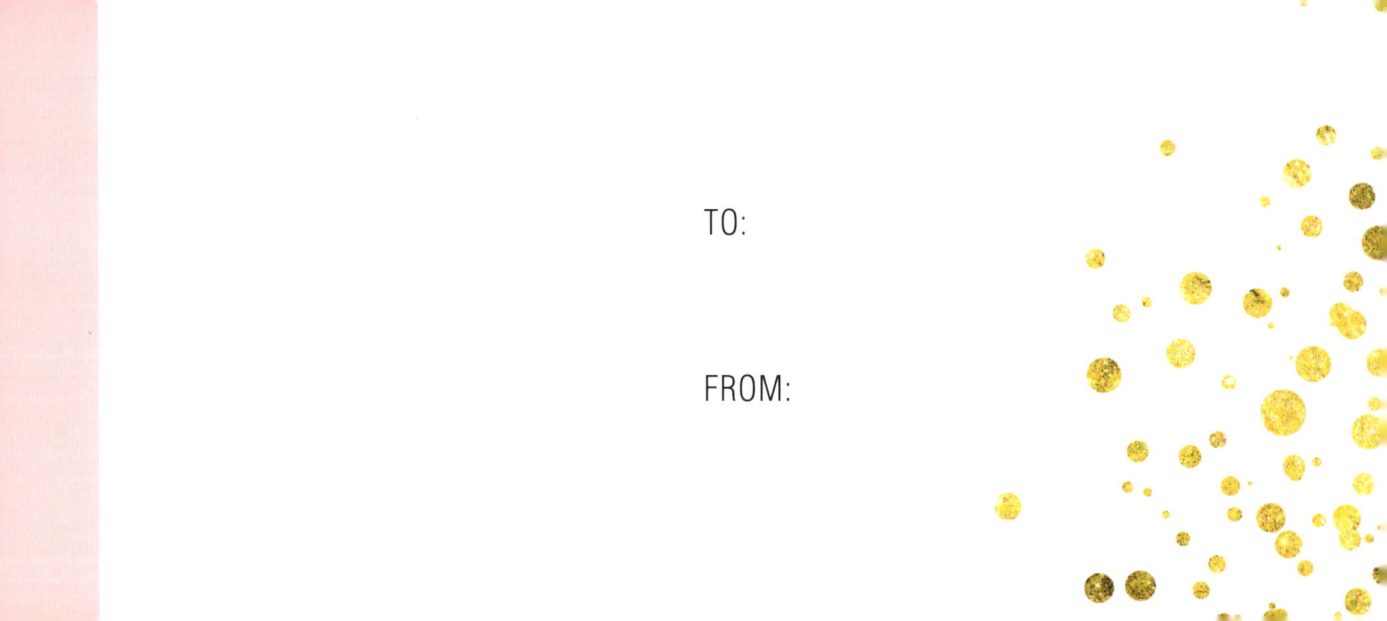

TO:

FROM:

# redeem this note

for some scintillating foreplay—for as long as you want, without rushing to the grand finale.

TO:

FROM:

It's

playtime!

Hand over this note and we'll role-play
whatever scene you desire.

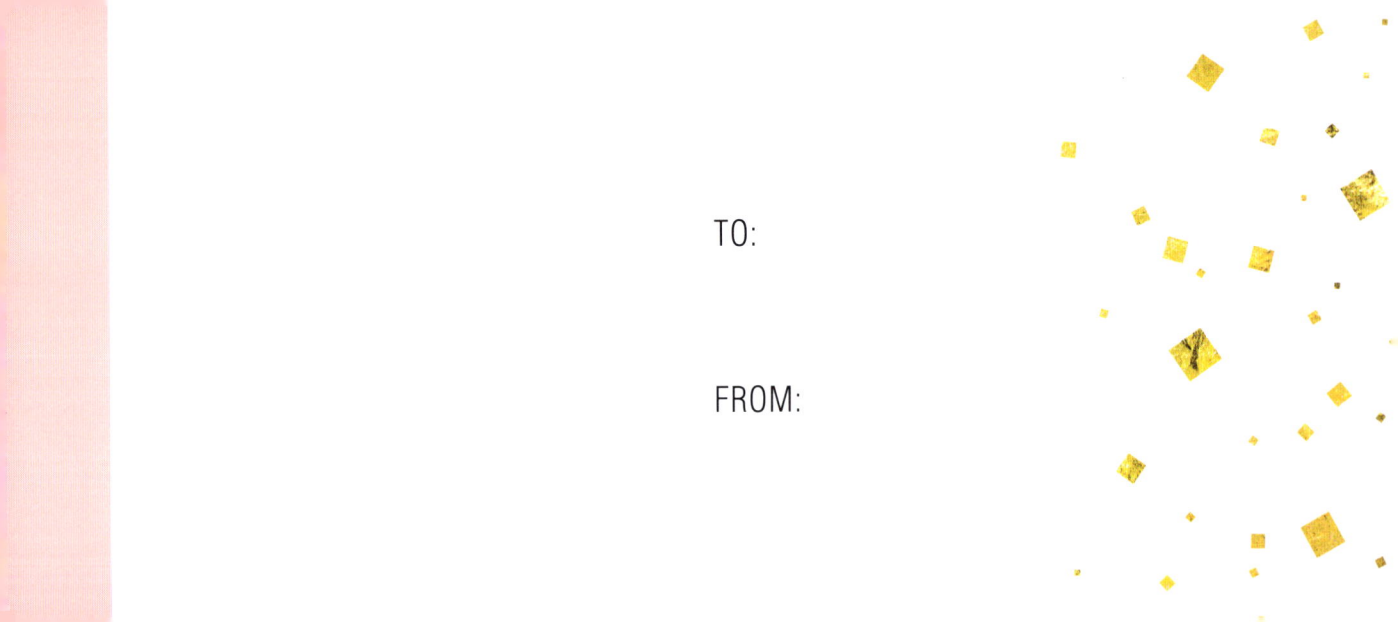

TO:

FROM:

Think of each word in this note as a kiss

*from my lips*

to your body.

TO:

FROM:

# redeem this note

for one game of strip poker—you name the time and place.

TO:

FROM:

# I love

getting you hot and bothered.

Hand over this note for a steamy shower with me on my knees.

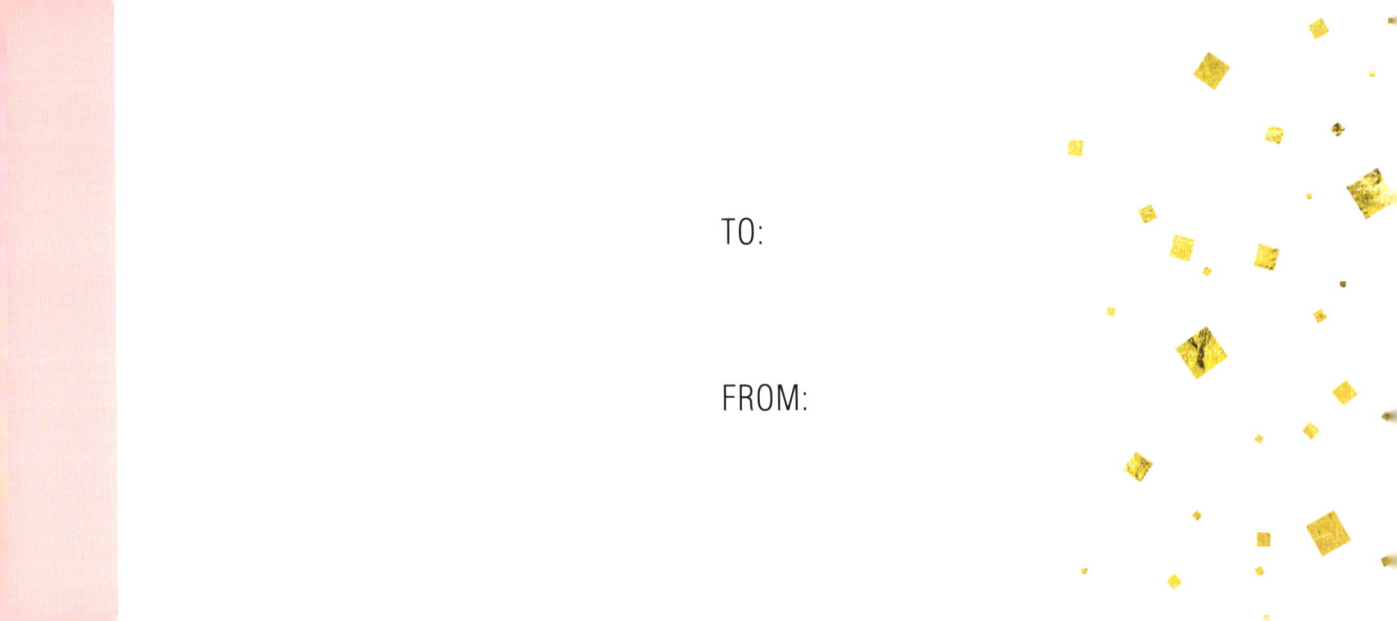

TO:

FROM:

From the top of your head to the tip of your toes,

*I adore kissing*

every inch of you.

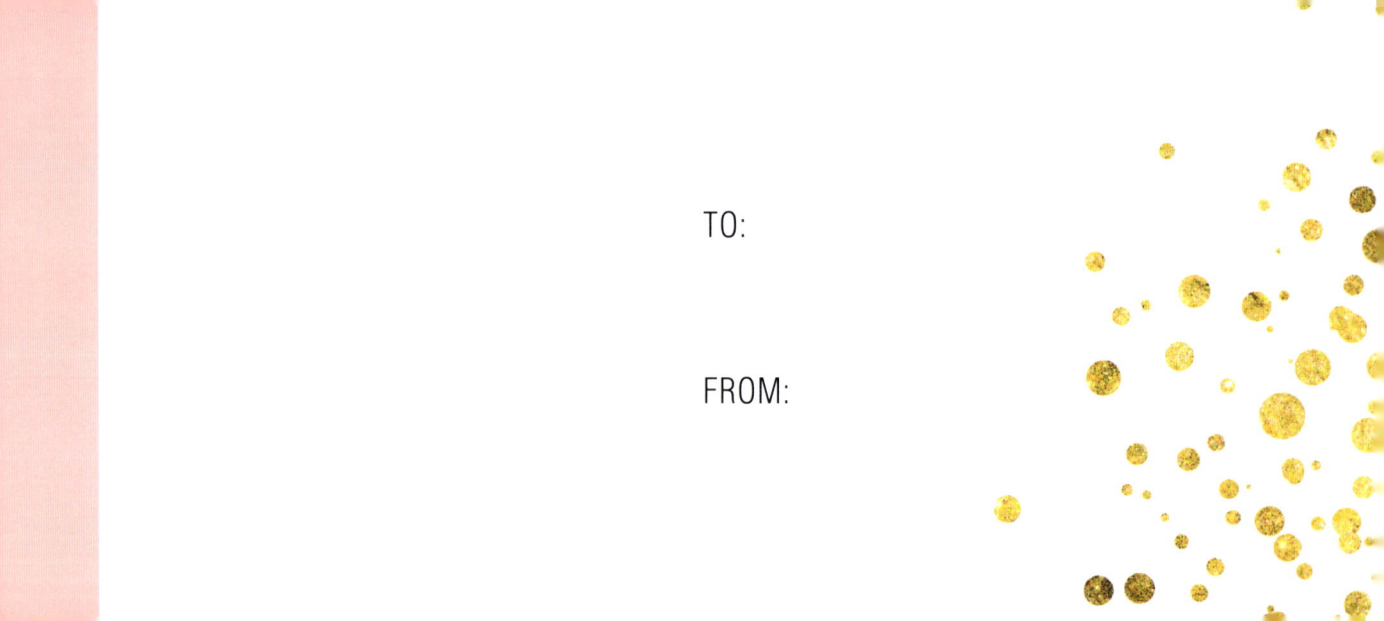

TO:

FROM:

# redeem this note,

and I'll do a little striptease for your eyes only.

TO:

FROM:

# I want you

so badly, I'm always ready.

Hand over this note when you're longing for a morning quickie.

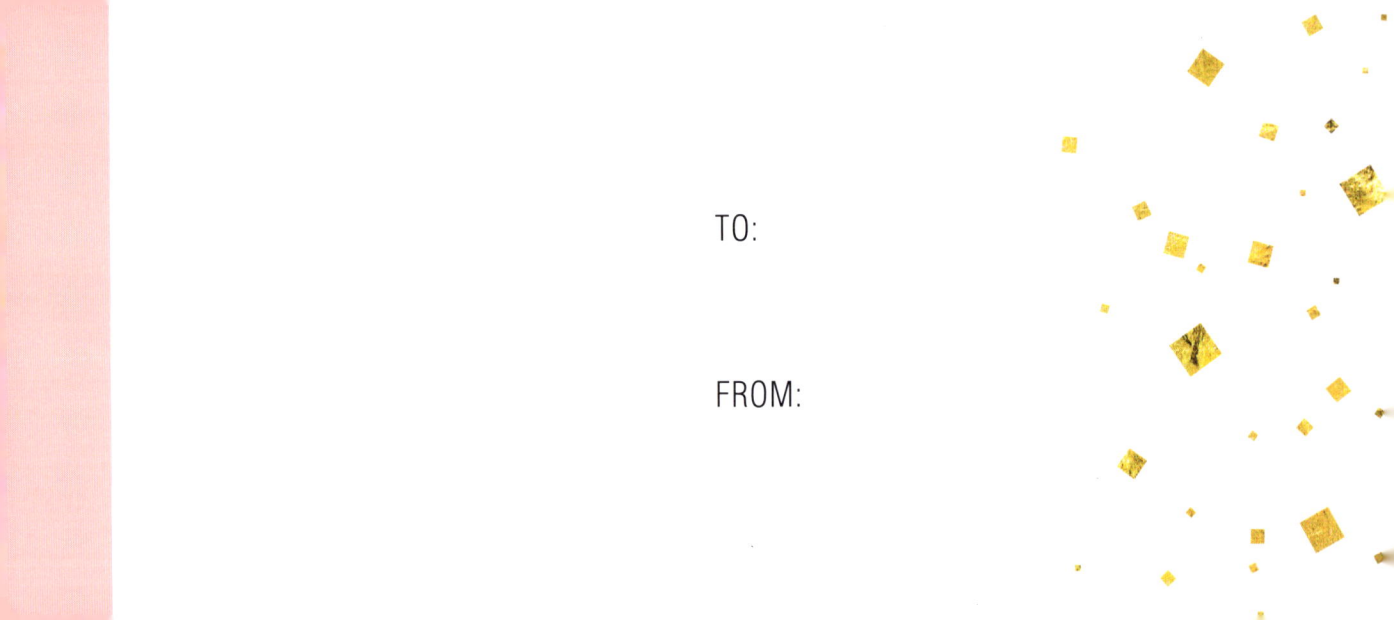

TO:

FROM:

You make me want to

*stay in bed*

all day just so I can be with you.

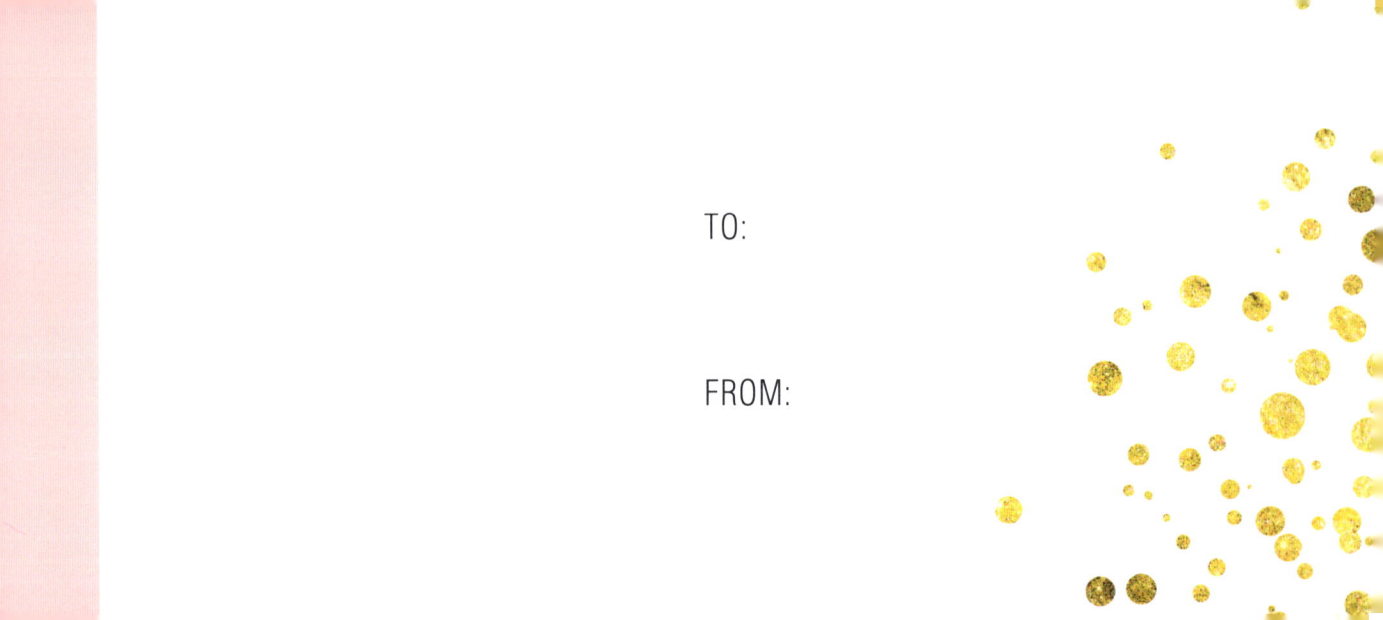

TO:

FROM:

# redeem this note,

and I'll whisper in your ear until you can't take it any longer.

TO:

FROM: